ISA Eternal Brotherhood

TAMING YOUR DARKNESS

ISA Eternal Brotherhood

THE ABOUT

The ISA Eternal Brotherhood - Sithdom Aliances is a Brotherhood of likeminded individuals that call themselves Sith. Some may join the Alliances and see Sithdom as a religion while others call it a philosophy, but to all brethren of the Empire, it is home. This book will be the second edition and the final "guide" work of the Imperial Sithdom Alliances. Through the pages of this text, we will work together to uncover truths, learn histories, and forge young minds into Darths of the Empire.

ISA Eternal Brotherhood

Disclaimer

The ISA (Imperial Sithdom Alliances) is not affiliated, associated, authorized, endorsed by, or in any way connected with The Walt Disney Company, Disney Enterprises, Inc., or any of its subsidiaries or its affiliates. The official Disney Website is available at www.disney.com.

The information within this book is purely for inspirational and educational purposes based on ISA standards and should be regarded for religious and philosophical purposes.

ISA Eternal Brotherhood

Chapters

1 BASICS

Why we become Sith

The Sith Code

Pillars of Sithdom

ISA creed

Laws of Sithdom

2 HISTORIES

Our Beginnings

The great Schisms

2000 -1000 BBY: Brotherhood of Darkness

Darth Bane and the Rule of Two

3 DEEPER STUDIES

Understanding the Sith Code

Taking an apprentice

Exploring the Force

Meditation

ISA Eternal Brotherhood

4 SITH MARAUDERS COLLECTION

The Lightsaber

Lightsaber Mechanics

Lightsaber Hilts

Synth Vs Kyber crystals

Lightsaber Forms

OPENING SITH QUOTE

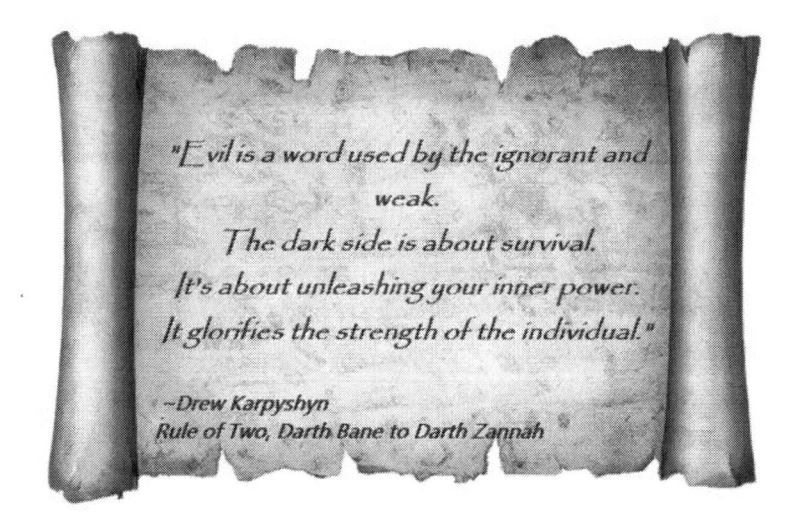

*"Evil is a word used by the ignorant and weak.
The dark side is about survival.
It's about unleashing your inner power.
It glorifies the strength of the individual."*

~Drew Karpyshyn
Rule of Two, Darth Bane to Darth Zannah

CHAPTER 1:

BASICS

ISA Eternal Brotherhood

WHY DO WE BECOME SITH?

We are Sith because we need to see life as it is. Black or white there is no gray. There is no ulterior choice in the matter for us. Some of us may find ourselves identifying as Sith because of the way our lives have gone. Some desire something more out of life but the reasons do not matter as we all have found ourselves in similar predicaments along the way. There is one reason above all that drives an individual to be Sith and that is "Security." It is human nature to seek out three main things in life: strength, power, and knowledge. Because these three things exist together in a triumvirate. But what it boils down to in a single word is, "SECURITY" We seek it. We need it.

What is Power to you?

The Dictionary would provide you with two basic definitions.

1.) The ability to do something or act in a particular way, especially as a faculty or quality.

>   2.) The capacity or ability to direct or influence the behavior of others or the course of events.

But what is it you hope to gain from such power? Is it Power over others or power over your own life? These are normal questions to ask of our own humanity though it takes focus to find the answers and the results you seek. Together we shall explore this together.

What is life without focus? The focus on what our own inner desires are and how to focus our strengths and desires on wanting more. Without these very desires we would be stuck in a mediocre society and despite what many of us are taught as children with second place trophies or participation ribbons, sadly that is not the world we live in and there is not a second place for life. Either you will ultimately succeed, or you will fail, that is the hard truth about life. Once you reach a certain age nobody is going to coddle you, nobody asks you anymore, "what is your favorite dinosaur?" No, those days of innocence slowly disappear.

It does not matter if you're a CEO of a multi–million-dollar empire or a fast-food worker we all eventually want more. This is the inner desire for power that whispers to us all and tugs at our very essence begging to be fed, it is the system that tells us to accept the human condition and to accept the way things are and not to challenge the status quo or not to want more. But that is not human nature, is it? Humans inherit a survival instinct the dates to cave man to branch out and secure more in doing so we adapt to a coveting state. Whether it is your neighbor's wife, the raise at work, the fancy Lamborghini that so few of us will ever have the money to ever even touch. Now of course we are not telling you to go out and be Sith like in the movies and take what you want because it is part of the human condition, and we are Sith. However, to be Sith is to see the holes and to understand that things are not always as they appear, and it is okay to want and desire more. It is okay to give yourself permission to seek out your desires and to go for what you want in life.

But what makes us so much different than other

individuals? What makes a Sith who they are, is it their mentality or is it something psychological perhaps?

A Sith is roughly defined by Star Wars as Dark Siders who are antagonists driven only by their own selfish emotions. But to better understand who you are you must look deeper inside. Often the deeper we explore ourselves and what it means for who we are, we will find more than the answers we were seeking. It is important to know before an individual begins their journey of who they are; more times than not those answers we find are ugly and can be rooted in fear. It is important that we confront this fear head on and challenge it. Accepting that we all have fear and insecurity inside is the only way we can challenge and overcome these obstacles before they weigh us down and become weak. One cannot hope to move on or achieve greatness in life if they are constantly weighed down in self-doubt or insecurity that is why it is one of the first steps of being Sith. Weakness is something a Sith cannot abide as it will cripple you in your own personal development. A true Sith will cut out and destroy

weakness before it destroys themselves. For only a True Sith will recognize that they must be true to their nature in accepting...
STRENGTH, POWER, and VICTORY.

It Is most Important In our development and growth as Sith to recognize what drew us into the Darkness and why we are at the precipice in life that we need this great strength and power. For some of us the need for such is the equivalent of the need and feeling to survive life itself. For others it is the feeling of necessity and desire to crave power. Something in life has pushed us to the edge and over the deep in; Be it loss, pain, abuse, neglect, fear of the unknown etc. Something has happened to shake our lives that has driven us in a different direction.

To quote a famous movie:

"Life is pain highness. Anyone who says different is selling something."

~Princess Bride

Indeed, this is a true statement. And often it is a

lesson here that leads us into the path of Sithdom and with that into the desire for more security. But how does one deal with everyday pain? Certainly, one can learn to accept life, to roll with the punches, to roll over and become a sheep but that is what makes us so much more different the others. We refuse to go down without a fight we and find ways to survive through other means when necessary.

Some people would argue that, currently, almost anyone could be considered Sith. This might be true except for one thing. People want to believe in something good and often righteous. This can give people a sense of hope in a world of pain and suffering and in such a world, hope can be a blessing and a curse all depending on how you look at things. A Jedi may choose to look at a glass half full and see that there is always hope in how we can make the world a better place. However, false hope can be a dangerous thing; limiting an individual's potential and ability to achieve greatness by achieving victory over their own personal trial and tribulations that life may have pushed on them. For when we begin to thrust false forget hope, we forget to trust ourselves and we accept things as they are which invites in mediocrity. False hope and being trapped by the simplicity of life is what separates us from the average person and how a Jedi chooses to live and think.

~FALSE HOPE~

"Blessed are the destroyers of false for they are the true messiahs -
Cursed are the god adorers, for they shall be shorn sheep."

~Anton Lavey

"Harsh Reality is better than false hope."

~Julian Fellows

> "I don't know when it will be, but someday... I will conquer it. And I will do it without... False Hope."
>
> ~*FFX (2001 Video Game) Yuna*

But why do we ultimately choose the path of Sithdom? Is it out of necessity to relinquish ourselves from our fear and insecurities or do we secretly desire more strength and power or is it a culmination of all the above because it is our fears and insecurities that make us want and desire more than the most?

Fear, Hate, and Anger are the three leading attributes that put us on the path of Sithdom. The passion of our past is what drives us to the decisions of our future. Not everyone will allow their emotions to drive them forward, but there are some of us that grow tired of the situations we find ourselves in or the way life has done us. The only are some of us that seem to be born into a life of pain and darkness and the only way we find our way is by adopting hate and anger to survive.

What separates us from the rest of mediocre society is the fact that we refuse to give into defeat. One might call us warriors, but what is a warrior and what makes us different from the average warrior's attributes?

A warrior is defined as a person who is often experienced in warfare and pledges him or herself with honor and often to another cause or conflict. A Sith may be trained as a warrior but often only cares inwardly for their own desires and personal needs. It is this that separates us from the average warrior and man. We think inwardly about the pain that has been done to us in life and we choose to use this hurt to influence our own emotions to empower us to push forward and strive to greatness.

But what drives us to become this way?

Is it psychological? Some would argue, yes. Perhaps it is or perhaps it is that we have seen darkness at such a young age we have had to adapt our lives into darkness because we have become accustomed to such pains and suffering. But whatever the reason, all those that sincerely search for the darkness in hopes to control it suffer from two things above all, fear and insecurity. And before you start making excuses and try to turn your head from such an idea, we invite you to really reflect on what is being said. What is insecurity other than doubt we place on ourselves due to life's circumstances. It is just another chain that we must look at to be broken and achieve the power we seek.

THE SITH CODE

> Peace is a lie, There is only passion.
> Through Passion, I gain strength.
> Through Strength, I gain power.
> Through Power, I gain Victory.
> Through Victory, my chains are broken.
> The Force shall free me.
> (The Sith Code)

UNDERSTANDING THE BASICS

Peace is a lie, there is only Passion.

Peace is a lie. Despite the dogmatic view of the jedi, peace can never be obtained not as they would see it. It is an impossibility; that even the universe itself would be in constant battle and at odds with itself if such a kind of peace were truly obtainable.

There is only passion. It speaks to us about the passion of life and what drives us onward with our innermost desires.

Through passion, I gain strength.

It is our passions that drive us forward in life and through these passions of that we discover our truest of strengths. Strengths are often revealed to us at the strangest of times when we feel we are the weakest or that we could give up, it is at that time through our passions that we gain strength.

Through strength, I gain power.

It is through our inner strength or strength discovered and gained through life's tribulations that we realize that we have the power. It is through all the pain, anger, suffering, and other paths to the dark side that we find ourselves finally faced with power. It then becomes clear, take it, it's yours. And it is through your strength that you gain power.

Through Power, I gain Victory.

It is our struggles that teach us strength and power and through this we can gain victory over our lives and whatever challenges may dare try to impede us on our journey to success.

Through Victory, my chains are broken.

Our personal victory over life and our personal chains that bind us are set free from us. It is only through the code that we may be free.

The Force shall Free me.

We as sith learn we do not work alongside the force, but rather it serves us while we take control of our destiny and our lives thus securing us to victory. In this, the force sets us free to all the things that bound us from before.

The full version of the Sith Code :
(Extended)

There is no peace, there is anger
There is no fear, there is power
There is no death, there is immortality
There is no weakness, there is the Dark Side.

I am the heart of darkness
I know no fear
But rather I instill it in my enemies
I am the destroyer of worlds
I know the power of the Dark Side
I am the fire of hate.

All the universe bows before me
I pledge myself to the darkness
For I have found true life
In the death of the light.

Peace is a lie, there is only passion.
Through passion, I gain strength.
Through strength, I gain power.
Through power, I gain victory.

ISA Eternal Brotherhood

> Through victory, my chains are broken.
> The Force shall free me.

The Sith Code Translated into the Sith Language

Pakor kash zur, sa ank kas
Dor kas, Ja'ty An'hin
Dor An'hin, Ja'ty Ar'rii
Dor Ar'rii, Ja'ty venaal
Dor venaal, Ja'ak
Plag Kaaran, Va Ja'ak

(This particular translation was done by Founder and Creator, Rena Mingus –
Sith Cosplay Club Sith Dynasty)

Though many of us choose just to take the bottom part of the extended Sith code as what we memorize and take with us. Our code is often used as a greeting among one another "Peace is a lie." This is used to show that we are Sith and is also a way to identify one another. Another Sith should and will respond with the next line, "There is only Passion." Or some may say the rest of the Sith code. But no matter which Sith code is decided to be used and committed to heart whether the extended or the last section one thing remains the same and that is what it means to us as Sith.

Our Sith Code is not meant to be taken as something small to read over but the very foundation for who we are. If you take the time to study the words and to live the meaning you will begin to fully understand the words themselves are more of a map for us to study and to find our way as true Sith.

We will delve deeper into the code's meaning later withing the pages of this book and text.

PILLARS OF SITHDOM

From the Sith Code that all those identify as Sith know comes the Pillars of the Sith Code which should be identified as the following

Strength   Power   Victory

But why in this order and why did the ISA Sith Empire adopt these as its fundamentals and as their Tenets?

Simple answer because these are the only things listed within the Code which might be gained and harnessed. They are the path to Power in and over all things.

CREED

We are the Sith-

Where we see chaos, We command Order.
Where there is Pain, We summon Strength.
Where there Darkness, We create Power.
Where there are enemies, we triumph in Victory.

We are the Sith-

Through our darkest days we will see Passion.
Through our Passions we will find Deliverance.
Within our Deliverance we will be triumphant in

Strength, Power, and Victory.

For we are the Sith, may our ambitions and enemies kneel to our power.

LAWS OF SITHDOM

The laws of Laws of Sithdom are 10 basic principles that have been created to help sith stay steadfast and true in their journey in following the code and ensuring Victory over their life over their life no matter the trials they may face. May these laws exist as guides to help you know and reflect on what path may assist you in the dark side.

- Know and understand the history which brought you to the Darkness.
- Accept change and alterations as they are a part of life.
- Do not fight scenarios which are put before you but instead accept fate to control and mold your own destiny.
- Live, Breathe, and Follow the tenets of being a Sith so that you may taste power and live free from the chains that once bound you.

- Accept deceptions are a part of life- enemies wear different masks for that always be aware of your surroundings and the people in your vicinity.
- Learn to read an enemies' lies so that you are never taken off guard.
- Learn the way of deception and subterfuge. The best deception is spoken with 80 percent truth, 20 percent lies.
- Always be Polite even to one's enemy, this alone may take them off guard when they least expect an attack.
- Always keep a multitude of plans, but never share your inner ambitions lest they be used against you.
- Age old saying, "Keep your friends close and your enemies closer." Even a brother one may one day hold a dagger at your back.

ISA Eternal Brotherhood

End of chapter review:

1.) What is the number one thing that leads us to seek out power?

2.) What are some of your personal insecurities and where do they stem from?

3.) What caused these insecurities in life?

4.) What are some of your triggers that cause you to go into rage seeking more power?

5.) What are some of your personal goals that will help you achieve strength and power to overcome weakness, fears, and any insecurities?

6.) What are the pillars of the Sith Code?

7.) Through what and how are the pillars achieved?

8.) Think of scenarios in which the laws of Sithdom can be useful in life to success or to prevent loss of victory.

CHAPTER 2:
HISTORIES

OUR BEGINNINGS

Our Dark History is shrouded in darkness, betrayal, and pain.
Yoda once said, "Fear is the path to the dark side. Fear leads to anger. Anger leads to hate. Hate, leads to suffering." This quote is stated by one of the most well-known and strong Jedi and it could not be any truer.
But was he speaking in general or is this true to all facts of life? Did Yoda realize he was speaking to the fact of the very creation of Sith as well?

Our Dark History begins with the betrayal of the Jedi over the Sith.
Most of us are already familiar with the history and the beginnings of the Sith. But for those of you who are new I will touch base so that you may understand the betrayal.
We who call ourselves Sith were all once considered Jedi. Eons of betrayal stain our blood with the betrayal of our polluted beginnings.

The Sith line begins with Ajunta Pall who began as a Jedi Master following the First Great Schism approximately 130,000 BBY. Ajunta Pall would be the first among many, the first Dark Jedi to turn on the ways of the Jedi deciding that there was much more to the force than the light side teachings. The Dark Jedi was known to be an expert in Alchemy and reached such levels he became known to have discovered ways of creating and shaping life. It was such an ability that drove the narrow-minded Jedi to betrayal stating such was an abomination to the way of the Jedi and the light side of the force. Seeking to end such studies, fearful of what it might mean. Such a decision left Ajunta Pall and so a war began against the Jedi (The One Hundred Year Darkness) Throughout this war Ajunta Pall grew in power and strength slaying many Jedi and is known that he killed over a dozen Jedi during the final battle of the Hundred Year Darkness on Corbos. But despite Ajunta Pall and his followers' efforts during this war, the Hundred Year Darkness came to a halt they were captured and stripped of all weapons and ranks under the Jedi and were cast out from the Galactic Republic.

After Ajunta Pall and his followers became cast out from the Galactic Republic they sought their sights to the outer rim planets and came across Korriban, a desert wasteland inhabited by a primitive species compared to that of the Dark Jedi and found that the inhabitants had the ability to tap strongly into the dark side of the force. Among these primitives on Korriban was Hakagram Graush, the King of the Sith. Ajunta Pall being Dark Jedi and seeking more power attempted to subjugate the Sith to obtain the knowledge for himself and the rest of his followers. Though the king originally thwarted the Dark Jedi's attempts, Ajunta Pall was able to succeed in luring the King's Shadow Hand to their side leading to the ultimate betrayal and execution of Hakagram Graush.

…Over Time the Natives of Korriban began to look upon Ajunta Pall and his followers as Gods and named Ajunta Pall, Jen'ari. "Dark Lord" Ajunta Pall established the first Sith Empire and expanded their rule over many planets claiming Ziost as their Capital.

THE GREAT SCHISMS

There are Four great Schism in the Histories. Each Schism speaks to several different issues that lead to a great war between the Sith and the Dark Jedi who later were made to be known as Sith.

1. The First Great Schism: The Legions of Lettow; First breakaway from the Jedi

2. The Second Great Schism: The Following of Ajunta Pall and the One Hundred Year Darkness

3. Third Great Schism: Leading to the Vultar Cataclysm

4. Fourth Great Schism (The Great Schism): The Jedi launch a crusade to reclaim the Sith worlds

The first Schism dates back before the time of Ajunta Pall under the first Breakaway from the Jedi. As long as the Jedi have been, they have always tried enforcing their dogmatic beliefs upon others and the force sensitives. The Schism takes place over Xendor becoming increasingly tiresome of the Jedi's narrow mindedness and ever exclusive ways in the force. He sought to further his knowledge and went to the Jedi Council seeking permission to open another academy far from Ossus, the Jedi Home world so that he may explore and study the darker sides of the force. Though his request was denied he would quietly break free of the jedi and establish an Academy on Lettow. There Xendor would focus his teachings on the Bogan, a group of dark jedi that broke from the neutral teachings of the force. It was the Jedi that initiated the battle and war as they grew tired of the continuous descendants falling from their ways.

The Second Great Schism is the beginning of our lineage as the Sith thanks be to Ajunta Pall.

The Third Great Schism takes place in 4250 BBY. For the third time, a group of descendants fall from the ways of the Jedi and turn to the Dark Side.

Though much of the time and information to us is lost during this great schism we know that after a long time of waiting the Dark Jedi were forced to retreat into an area known as the Vultar System. Whilst in the Vultar system a great technology was discovered that was believed to be able to hold a power so great as to artificially create planets. During the use of trying and controlling the machines a horrible misfortune arose as a malfunction so great struck later came known to be the Vultar Cataclysm, The entire annihilation of the Vultar System.

The Fourth Great Schism takes precedence when the Jedi Master Phanius seeks more power and falls from the way of the Jedi seeking out the once great Sith in 2000 BBY. The now Dark Jedi successfully finds the remnants of the once great Sith throughout the galaxy and declares himself to be Dark Lord over the Sith after uniting the Sith Clans under the new identity of Darth Ruin. The ascension of the new Sith Lord Ruin prompts the following of fifty other Jedi to leave the light side and thus begins the thousand years war from 2000 BBY to 1000BBY leading to the time of the Brotherhood of Darkness lead by Kaan.

2000 – 1000 BBY: BROTHERHOOD OF DARKNESS

In the year 2000 BBY not long after the Fourth Great Schism. When the ranks of the Jedi order split, Former Jedi Master Phanius (Darth Ruin), abandoned the ways of the Jedi in pursuit of alternate teachings, leading him on a quest to revive the dark side worshiping Sith Order, by this point, the Sith were commonly believed to have been destroyed for centuries.

The fallen Jedi Master proved otherwise however, seeking out existing Sith clans throughout the galaxy. Prompted by the Dark Lord's ascension, fifty additional Jedi chose to follow in Ruin's footsteps, leaving the Jedi Order in favor of his growing Sith empire, these events gave rise to the New Sith, initiating a thousand-year-long crusade—the New Sith Wars—against the Galactic Republic and the Jedi.

The New Sith Wars, also known as the Jedi–Sith War, and known to the Sith as the War of the Fittest, The Betrayal and The Curse of Qalydon, was the name given to the thousand years of conflict between the

Jedi and the Sith, which lasted from approximately 2000 to 1000 BBY.

As an era, the New Sith Wars were characterized by a spectacular rise of the Sith, the decline of the Galactic Republic, and a growing militancy in the Jedi Order. The balance between the Sith and the Republic fluctuated during the period, and at several periods, especially after the pivotal Battle of Mizra, the Republic was in danger of being overwhelmed completely.

In 1466 BBY during the battle of Mizra and unnamed Sith Sniper shot the Jedi Coordinator during his battle meditation these actions resulted in a large scale (500,000 troops) slaughter of the Jedi. This battle was a Major Sith Victory, resulting in the capture of many outer rim territories and provoking mass Jedi defections.

The New Sith Wars was coinciding with the Draggulch Period of galactic history and the Sictis Wars. Leading to this era becoming commonly known as the Republic dark Age, and the name Light and Darkness War was sometimes specifically applied to the final series of battles between the Sith Brotherhood of Darkness and the Jedi Army of Light. The reign of Darth Ruin ended prematurely due to the Instigation of his backstabbing followers, setting a treacherous precedent that would plague his successors for many centuries. Nonetheless, the New Sith had emerged into a bloody age of galactic expansion, eventually giving rise to a new leader.

In around 1750 BBY, a dark side spirit known as the "Dark Under-lord" reigned as a Dark Lord of the Sith. A shadowy figure of unknown origins, the Dark Under-lord was a male Sith warlord who rose to leadership over the revived Sith empire, establishing an alliance known as the Black Knights. Based on the planet Malrev IV, the Under-lord led a bloody campaign against the Galactic Republic and the Jedi Order, terrorizing the galaxy's Outer Rim Territories. These activities provoked the ire of Murrtaggh, a Jedi Master who, aided by Mandalorian mercenaries, misdirected the Black Knights in a surprise attack against the Under-lord's base of operations. This drove the Dark Under-lord into a personal confrontation with Murrtaggh himself, during which the Sith Lord met his ultimate demise against the Jedi Master, promptly ending the Dark Lord's reign. The death of the Dark Under-lord had an immediate impact on Jedi Master Murrtaggh, who fell to the dark side upon slaying the Dark Lord of the Sith. Despite the Under-lord's demise, the Sith crusades not only remained undeterred, but grew more dominant over the following centuries of the New Sith Wars. Additionally, the Black Knights, although defeated, reformed their numbers on several occasions in the absence of their fallen master. Following the eventual Sith defeat at the conclusion of the New Sith Wars, the Black Knights remained active during a conflict known as the Fluwhaka revolt.

In the wake of this upturn, the tyrannical Darth Rivan rose to leadership, creating a unique brand of warriors, the Battle lords, in an attempt to curb the string of betrayals among the Sith. This venture met an abrupt end, however, after Rivan and his Battle lords were entrapped, and ultimately destroyed, by a Sith artifact called the Dark staff.

The period from 1250 to 1230 BBY was known as the Sictis Wars. In that era, Belia Darzu ruled as Dark Lord of the Sith, unleashing Techno beasts, the Metanecrons, against the Jedi forces from her power base on Tython. The Sictis Wars came to an end with Darzu's death at the hands of the Mecrosa Order, who, though nominally allied with the Sith Empire, poisoned Darzu due to unwanted Sith incursions on Tapani territory.

Although the eleventh century BBY would later be described as the "Republic Dark Age," there is little evidence for any coherent Sith threat for much of the period. The Sith, though exponentially increased in number, were divided against one another in the Sith Civil Wars, as the various warlords and self-proclaimed Dark Lords fought each other for supremacy. These warlords squabbled over the dying embers of the Sith Empire, and while they remained divided, the Republic was given some respite. Some Jedi, such as Vannar Treece and his apprentice Kerra Holt would attempt daring raids within Sith-held territory, but for the most part the Republic made no attempt to regain its lost worlds.

Against the Sith threat, other members of the Jedi Order began quests to rout entire systems of Sith influence and purge those who's sought to enslave or exploit the citizens of the Republic. Standing as these systems' last line of defense, these individual Jedi became celebrated and quickly came to hold political might. As their constituent worlds came to appreciate their service, these Jedi became barons or kings of entire systems and sectors, taking up the title Jedi Lord, establishing castles and manors as their formal residences, these Lords created a formal hereditary system, passing down their titles to their offspring for several generations. The peaceful regions of space stood as islands of light in the darkness created by the Sith, and even Coruscant and the Galactic Senate was presided over by Jedi Supreme Chancellors. During this time, the Jedi High Council competed directly with the Jedi Grand Council which consisted of Lords from across the galaxy.

The Sith saw the crippled Republic"as a'sign that the Force was with them. However, their plans for a strike against Coruscant were halted after they fell into infighting over who would rule the galaxy after the Republic's defeat. An example of such internecine strife was the Charge Matrica of 1066 BBY in the Grumani sector. Owing to such fighting, the threat of the New Sith in the last century of the war was not as great as it might have been, and the Sith civil war would not end until 1010 BBY with the emergence of Lord Skere Kaan and the Brotherhood of Darkness.

In 1010 BBY, Skere Kaan, a Jedi Master who served the Jedi Order in the last years of the New Sith Wars before defecting to become a Dark Lord of the Sith and creating the Brotherhood of Darkness within the reorganized Sith Empire, earning him the nickname of the "Dark One". Ruling the Sith for a decade, Kaan's reign was turbulent as the Brotherhood was rife with civil unrest, and conflict with the Jedi saw his numbers dwindle. A few Sith were starting to question his beliefs, including Darth Bane.

Beginning in around 1010 BBY, this new group launched a series of attacks designed to destroy the Jedi and the Republic. Kaan, along with the two strongest of the former warlords, Qordis and Kopecz, began their campaign with a daring and symbolic assault on the ancient Sith home world of Korriban, which at that time was still under nominal Republic control. The successful capture of that world sealed their alliance and enabled the reopening of the ancient Sith academy under Qordis' leadership. As Qordis trained new recruits, Kaan and Kopecz continued their war, seizing worlds like Kashyyyk, and even briefly Corulag, Chandrila and Brentaal IV. By 1001 BBY, they seemed almost poised to conquer Coruscant, pressing the Republic on many fronts with the assistance of allies such as the turncoat Jedi King Lahzar, who battled the Republic in the Tholatin system and a colony of Chiss on Thule, abducted from the Unknown Regions by agents of Kaan.

However, Lord Hoth, a Jedi Master and Republic General, had been scoring victories of his own against the Sith. Driving the Brotherhood from their home in the heavily defended region of space known as the Cloak of the Sith, Hoth chased them from world to world, from Hoth to Dromund Kaas to Malrev IV. In many of his earlier campaigns, he commanded Republic fleets and armies, but around 1002 BBY, he forged the bulk of the Jedi Order's fighting strength into an independent military force known as the Army of Light.

The war ended with the armies of Hoth and Kaan facing each other on the world of Ruusan. Lord Hoth's army of was made of seven Legions of Light, each led by a Jedi Lord, including Valenthyne Farfalla, Gale, Saleeh, Teepo, Berethon, and Newar Forrth. Under the Jedi Lords served Jedi Generals such as Kiel Charny.

Kaan's Brotherhood was led by himself, Qordis, Kopecz and less familiar Dark Lords such as Seviss Vaa, LaTor and Githany. The Army of the Light and the Brotherhood of Darkness clashed seven times on the world, each battle causing terrible casualties as Sith and Jedi died in the thousands. Throughout the course of the battles, additional reinforcements attempted to land on Ruusan, though many Jedi forces were destroyed by an orbiting Sith blockade and many Sith reinforcements were destroyed by the Republic Navy en route to Ruusan. Though four of the seven battles were won by the Army of Light, their casualties were still enormous, and the campaign would later be considered the deadliest clash between Jedi and Sith in galactic history. Dissension was rife in both camps – for the Jedi, Hoth feuded with his fellow Lord Valenthyne Farfalla, a rift which only deepened with the death of Pernicar, a Jedi Master who had mediated between the two Lords. Even when Farfalla arrived with over three hundred fresh knights as reinforcements, having both defeated the traitorous King Lahzar and broken the Sith blockade over Ruusan, Hoth still refused to speak to him. The Jedi were further undermined when a recruit, Darovit, turned traitor murdering General Charny and defecting to the Sith.

Among the Sith, Kaan's leadership began to be questioned by both Githany and Kopecz, and Kaan's bungled attempt to remove his rival Darth Bane only served to make him seem foolish, especially after Bane defeated Qordis, Kaan's strongest supporter. Bane mocked Kaan's reliance on traditional weapons of war and goaded the Sith leader into using the dark side of the Force to destroy Hoth and the Jedi. With Bane's help, Kaan and the other Dark Lords devastated the unprepared Jedi with a Force Storm that ravaged Ruusan's surface.

Finally, with both armies nearly destroyed, and the once lush planet totally devastated, the seventh and final Battle of Ruusan took place, ending with Kaan's decision to use an ancient Sith technique known as the thought bomb, the instructions secretly provided by Darth Bane in a plot to destroy the other Sith Lords and leave Bane to rebuild the Sith under the "Rule of Two." To dissuade Kaan from unleashing the weapon, Lord Hoth, knowing of his opponent's final gambit, took 99 of his most trusted knights with him and confronted the Sith Lord. His friend, Tal attempted to dissuade him, having seen disaster through the Force. Lord Farfalla did likewise, but Hoth told both that Kaan had to be stopped.

At the end of the bloody Ruusan campaign, Kaan, his followers, and much of the Jedi Army of Light were destroyed by a thought bomb of his own creation during the Seventh Battle of Ruusan. The Jedi and the Republic prepared themselves for a future of peace and prosperity, with the Sith nothing more than a painful memory of the past. This, however, was a dangerous delusion, as a single Sith, Darth Bane, had in fact survived. Bane formed a new Sith Order and he and his successors spent the next thousand years in hiding, waiting to topple the Republic once and for all. Darth Bane, who tricked the entire Brotherhood into its destruction, set up a new Sith order with the Rule of Two: one master and one apprentice.

Darth Bane, retreated from the carnage of Ruusan, finding a Force-sensitive child named Rain from among the child recruits of the Army of Light. After the final battle the pair escaped the effects of the thought bomb and made their way, separately, to Onderon. Bane would accept Rain as his apprentice, dubbing her Darth Zannah, and from her would continue an unbroken line of Sith Lords, culminating in Darth Sidious and Darth Vader, who achieved what the Sith of the past never could: the destruction of the Galactic Republic, and the near annihilation of the Jedi Order.

After a thousand years, the New Sith Wars had finally come to an end in 1000 BBY.

DARTH BANE AND THE RULE OF TWO

> "Two there should be; No more, no less. One to embody the power, the other to crave it."
> Drew Karpysyn – The Darth Bane Series

Darth Bane the creator of the Rule of Two was a legendary Sith Lord and Sith'ari who came into power after the Seventh Battle of Ruusan aka *The Battle of Ruusan*. The most important battle that took place on Ruusan that would judge the overall fate of the Republic. Though the Battle of Ruusan might have been able to be won and a victory over the Jedi could have secured the Sith's seat of power for the next thousand years, Darth Bane had other plans as he tricked Lord Kaan into use of the thought bomb. The thought bomb ultimately destroyed the Brotherhood of Darkness by trapping the essence of himself, the Brotherhood, Lord Hoth, and a great many Jedi into an orb.

Sith'ari: A terminology and title that originally was given to King Adas 27,700 BBY. Translated to mean perfect being or perfect god. A prophecy was formed after King Adas's death by the Kissai and recorded by Sorzus Syn 6,900 BBY.

The Sith'ari will be free of limits.
The Sith'ari will lead the Sith and destroy them.
The Sith'ari will raise the Sith from death and make them stronger than before.

Thought Bomb: The origins of this date back to the Ritual of Nathema by the ancient Sith. A mystical vortex created by the joining of a multitude of Sith Lords' will power that traps their essence in an orb.

The Rule of Two was created to replace the Brotherhood of Darkness' assertion that all Sith were equal. Within the Rule of Two it was set that a Master would take one apprentice and pass their knowledge and skills along to their successor. By limiting the Sith's power between Master and apprentice the Sith could focus more on their goals and work from the shadows without the Jedi's focus. Moreover, the idea of the Rule of Two was so that the Sith could grow in strength and power over time.

*An apprentice would already have apparent abilities in the force which a Master would sharpen with their already previous learned abilities and powers from prior Masters. In doing this each apprentice would grow with their Masters' knowledge of those that came before them.

The Baneite lineage lasted for 1000 years from Master to apprentice.

"When your power eclipses mine I will become expendable. This is the Rule of Two: one

Master and one apprentice. When you are ready to claim the mantle of Dark Lord as your own, you must do so by eliminating me."

~Darth Bane to his apprentice Darth Zannah

End of Chapter Review

1.) How many Schisms are there?
2.) What are the major Schisms?
3.) Who was the first Dark Lord of the Sith?
4.) What are the key events that led to the destruction of the Brotherhood of Darkness?

CHAPTER 3:
DEEPER STUDIES

ISA Eternal Brotherhood

UNDERSTANDING THE SITH CODE

One of the most important things that a Sith must learn is the Sith Code. But what is it about the Sith Code that makes it so important? Is it a religious piece, mantra, or just a bunch of philosophical words that indoctrinate an inner meaning? For Sithist or Realist the Sith Code can be a religious piece. For those that are beginners or use the code for meditation and assistance to master control would argue it is a Mantra. For individuals that are stuck between the realm of truly believing and respecting the ways of the Sith as a necessity and way of life would argue that the words have a philosophical meaning behind the words that we have learned to take to heart. However, the reason behind the existence of the words is not what is most important, instead the meaning is what guides individuals on their way to becoming Sith. Before one even begins their path into understanding and attempting to control the Darkness, they must learn the code and commit it to heart and mind and fully understand the meaning of the words. The Immortal words of the Sith Code should be spoken as if they were words of intent and purpose. For if you speak these words, you should have a clear understanding of their meaning and what they can lead you to if you allow them to.

Peace is a Lie, there is only Passion
Peace and calmness can never exist, only our raw emotions.   Passion = Emotion

Through Passion, I gain Strength
By using our emotions to guide us strength is obtainable.

Through Strength, I gain Power
By obtaining such a strength, we will be able to find the power within.

Through Power, I gain Victory
It is with the raw power that Victory over our adversities will be made possible.

Through Victory, my chains are broken
It is with each of our victories in life we can begin to shred our mortal coil and ties to our past fears and pain.

The Force shall free me.
Granted one has learned to follow, understand, and live by the code. A new since of control will be

granted to you and the force will become an ally as you will learn to control yourself and your surroundings "Universe."

After one learns the Code and understands its nature. One should be able to identify it for what it is, and the pillars found amongst the Sith Code. Many would confuse the three pillars of the code as passion, strength, power, and victory, but that is not true. To be a pillar of something, the object mentioned must be obtainable or it must be something that simply is. When breaking down the code Passion is simply stating emotion.

"Passion of life" Your emotions of life and what your emotions may represent and how you feel currently in life. What life has been for you, and what you hope to accomplish and take from life once you begin being a Sith. With that in mind one can review the pillars from another angle. After all, one cannot passion something and one cannot obtain passion. Our emotions which dictate our passions in life lay dormant wanting to come out as you take your steps forward into the path of Darkness. However, STRENGTH, POWER, AND VICTORY can be obtained, and they are the goals of every Sith. The three pillars should be at the heart and soul of every person that dares to call themselves a Lord of the Sith. In review of the Code "Passion" is the only thing we do not go ... "Through to obtain" it simply is.

There is only Passion (this simply exists within our life.
Through Passion – Strength (First Pillar)
Through Strength – Power (Second Pillar)
Through Power – Victory (Third Pillar)

Now that we have explored and have a deeper understanding of our code and how it guides it is important to review the proper uses of our Sith Code. The Sith Code is there as a test, a reminder, and even a greeting amongst our fellow brethren.

The Code should be used as a greeting among your brethren. "Peace is a Lie" In which the proper response is "There is only Passion or a Sith should respond further with the entirety of our code. We use this greeting to identify with each other or hail in a manner of respect. It acts as a universal understanding that all Sith hold a great honor for.

ISA Eternal Brotherhood

A threat, the Sith Code can also be used as a threat against the Jedi before challenging our enemy to a dual. Stating such words to a Jedi "Peace is a lie" is an automatic threat and afront to state I am here, I am Sith and you should use caution or prepare for battle.

A Reminder, A Sith Mater to his apprentice will often use the words of the Sith Code as a teaching moment and method to remind his or her apprentice on the guidelines within and that they can be used to correct a behavior and remind the apprentice of who they are… "Sith."

TAKING AN APPRENTICE

The finding and taking of the correct apprentice may be one of the most difficult and time-consuming obstacles a Sith Lord may go through. In such, finding a correct match to teach what you have learned can often lead to trial and error. Much of this process is making sure the Sith Lord/apprentice dynamic is right for you. And it truly depends on what the Master has to offer and what the apprentice desires to learn. This dynamic focuses on a great deal of things such as one's own thoughts as a Sith and their own beliefs.

- Is the individual a Banite, someone following the Rule of Two and is looking for a successor.
- Is the Master looking for a partner, someone to learn together with and explore the darkness with.
- Is the Master strictly looking for loyalty in an apprentice. Someone to do their bidding and carry on their name.

- The Master is strictly looking to teach their thoughts, beliefs, and Sithism. In such the Master may not have any ulterior motive.

What does one look for in an apprentice and how does one know when one has been found? First, one should look at themselves from an outside perspective.
Ask yourselves these questions.

1. Have you Mastered yourself and the control which is needed in your own daily life?
2. Are you a Master of your own surroundings?
3. Have you Mastered an understanding of the Force and what that means to you as well as what the Darkness means to a Sith?

Only if you can answer yes to all the questions above are you probably ready to take on an apprentice and teach them the ways of the Sith and how to live in the Darkness. Know that you are ready to choose an apprentice, however if you are still questioning your path and your thoughts as well as wondering if you should take on an apprentice know that you should stop and rethink. The taking on an apprentice is one of the greatest challenges a Sith may face as it takes a great deal of responsibility and focus. Only when you are for sure, steady enough in your path and only if you truly understand and recognize your journey is never truly over when it comes to learning are you truly ready for an apprentice. Even as you take on an apprentice you will learn from them as you teach and guide them, for learning never truly stops in life.

Now that you have realized that you are ready to take on an apprentice what should one look for in an individual that you are willing to make yours. As was mentioned prior there are many different reasons a Lord or Darth may choose to take on an apprentice. One should reflect and meditate over themselves to discover what those reasons are. Are you seeking an apprentice to fully pass on your knowledge or
are you feeling it is simply time to take on an apprentice because it is your duty as a Lord? Whether you are simply looking to share your

understandings and or findings with someone or You need a full-on successor to carry on your name and legacy there are a great many things to consider.

Often, the longer one is a Lord or a Darth they begin to feel a certain tiresome emotion that begins to eclipse them over their daily lives. But no matter the reason one may have for the desire to take on an apprentice there are ways and things to look at as you make this important decision in your journey.

"Choose someone as a successor and you will inevitably be succeeded.

Choose someone hungrier and you will be devoured.

Choose someone quicker and you won't dodge the blade at your back.

Choose someone with more patience and you won't block the blade at your throat.

Choose someone more devious and you'll hold the blade that kills you.

Choose someone more clever and you'll never know your end.

Despite these cautions, an apprentice is essential.

A Master without an apprentice is a Master of nothing."

~Darth Sidious

Using the following as a guide to approach and gain your successor.

1.) Keep in mind that the individual and apprentice you may choose is not too young, the younger they are not always the best. In fact, a younger person may change their mind several times in their path of life and is still not mature enough to take on such a responsibility and the willpower to commit fully to the darkness or the path of a Sith. Nor will they be able to grasp the meaning of such things as meditation and the force of a living universal energy. A Sith Lord needs to consider the age as well as the maturity of the individual they are thinking should become their apprentice.

2.) Is the individual willing to commit themselves fully and are they willing to work hard to obtain the strength and power that will lead them to victory.

3.) How close do they live to you, and will distance be an issue in the future? Depending on what you and your future apprentices' desires are to learn and what the apprentice should learn will hold much sway over this factor. A Master should recognize that eventually an apprentice should be willing and wanting to complete their training, in which some things can only be accomplished in proximity.

*For some Sith Masters and apprentices these factors may be more important than others. This depends greatly on the reason for wanting to take an apprentice in the first place.   Some of these factors may be included.

- A Physical understanding and knowledge of weapons, lightsaber skills, and or martial arts.
- Understanding and the ability to recognize and use force is known to us as a universal energy. Be it through sorcery, and or basic manipulations such as aura readings etc.

4.)   What is the individual's reason for wanting to choose the darkness or the dark side. Ask the young one what their purpose or reason is to desire the path of becoming a Sith. An apprentice should respond with one of the following Power, Strength, or Knowledge. But always "Power" should be included in their answer. An individual who claims they desire knowledge should seek the library or other areas for reading. A person who only seeks strength should seek a gym. No answer for a young acolyte should ever be one of those without power accompanying their inner desire. Power is what a young Sith mind seeks and needs. They need this like they need air. For a Sith, Power is everything. Though there may be different reasons for their desire for power, and their environment. Only power can offer control over one's enemy.

"Tell me what you regard as your greatest strength, so I will know how best to undermine you;

Tell me of your greatest fear, so I will know which I must force you to face:

Tell me what you cherish most, so I will know what to take from you;

And tell me what you crave, so that I might deny you...

~Darth Plageuis

A relationship between a Master and an apprentice is a special one, but a challenging one. From the moment you accept your apprentice you play an exceptional role in that individual's life, from a mentor and a teacher to whatever solidifies the bond between the two. You will become somewhat responsible for your apprentice as they grow from an acolyte – apprentice and throughout their dark journey and if you are fortunate, you will see them reach Darth.

EXPLORING THE FORCE

What is the Force and how we as Sith see it?

The Force is a type of Universal Energy that connects the universe and all things living and even non. Unlike the Jedi, we as Sith see this as a power source which can be obtained and controlled. The Force itself as we know it is the energy which links time and space. Scientists would even seek to explain this connection in the way of atoms and molecules and that everything is made up of a living connection. In such there is no end to the Force, what it touches and or how it can be obtained.

History of Energy and the Force-

he terms of life force and life energy exists throughout the ages in multiple cultures and religions. Such practices were introduced as early as Ancient Egypt with ritual practices. Though during this time such prayers and ritual practices were more in a way to explore and explain the unknown. However, throughout the ages other civilizations and cultures have tapped into the understanding of what we call the force started to explore this phenomenon a bit more extensively and its understanding began to grow over time.

However, the terminology of life force did not technically become extremely popular until the eighteenth and nineteenth century which echoed into the Twentieth. Such that best describe are the concepts of Elan Vital and Qi. Elan Vital was best expressed in the 1907 book, Creative Evolution which best describes the development of organisms and evolution through time and space and the impact they have on individuals. Qi on the other hand comes from the Chinese culture expressing that there is a vital life force or energy which flows through all living things. The practice of Qi was also known to echo into medicine and even martial arts practices.

In some of our newer religions and practices introduced into the world are through those that practice magic and or the occult. In such they practice this through linking their personal energy through spells and incantations. Many of these individuals use material objects to amplify said energy into the universe and or other individuals.

Who is Most Sensitive?

If you follow the Star Wars lore and even study the concepts of energy and the force you will learn that not everybody is as sensitive to this phenomenon. It is said that energy or the force has its own vibration or signature that certain individuals can feel better than others. Those that are more sensitive to this phenomenon will often show certain traits, among these traits are the following.

- Empathic
- The ability to read crowded rooms for signs of trouble before others.
- The ability to read individuals and understand them on a mental and psychological level.
- Vivid dreams
- Predicting events or a sense of déjà vu
- Manipulating individuals by influencing other's emotions.

Learning to bond with the force-

When understanding the force and universal energy it is important to note that not everyone seems to understand or has a natural ability to tap into the source or even an inkling to comprehend the inner working of. Throughout time, energy has been a topic of debate between religions, cultural, and even scientific communities. As such the Imperial Sithdom Alliances do believe in the idea of the Force and that some are more inclined to access this rare universal phenomenon. Now, are we speaking the Force as described movies, "NO" let's go ahead and get that out of the way. However, how extraordinary would that be if a few of us possessed such abilities. But what we speak of as the force or a universal energy is something that can be tapped into like what has been described in so many religions that come before us by different names and described as spoken before "a universal energy" and with this universal energy we believe and note that all things in the universe are indeed connected. It is by exploring these secrets and these doorways into the subconscious that you can be able to control and the force and achieve great victories.

Depending on the course of seeking out this power would depend on the individual, some individuals tend to start off on a path that leans more in the occult.

The Occult is anything that factors in belief from the supernatural, magical, mystical, paranormal, and or witchcraft (sorcery) practices.

While it is known that many Sith learn to practice both Sith abilities and the occult there are multiple paths to help discover this.
Among these practices to understand and comprehend the force via the occult and the other sources are the following few.
(Following mentioned are not the only practices known to man) We have limited in this text for example purposes only.

Creating and developing an altar to raise your energy and practicing at (can be a place of worship and or self-reflection) An altar can be a place of solace and a place to summon or store energy. The ISA does not state that altars are necessary; nor do we advocate or forbid their uses. But we would post a warning for those that would use one for such practices. While they serve a good use for beginners, please note that altars can become a crutch to rely on for energy purposes and worship. *Worship as a Sith should be focused inwardly as a Sith to know who you are, where you come from, where you're going, and the victories in which you will achieve. It is for this reason that we suggest that only apprentices use altars unless you're a Lord or a Darth and rely on an altar for religious or ceremonial purposes.

Meditation (Reflection to yourself and your own surroundings through personal emotions and those around you.) The use of the word meditation is a way of strengthening one's thoughts and energy while learning to hone and concentrate on other energies that may be used to your advantage. *Use your own personal passions to stir and amplify your emotions to concentrate on your goals, desires, fears, pains, regrets, daily challenges, etc., to enhance your connection through the force.

Understanding elemental magicks. (Earth, air, fire, water, spirit) These types of practices are used by learning to control and manipulate the five basic elements of the universe or rather this plane's elements which are limited to the planet. This idea of energy gathering is a practice usually done by pagans and there is a limit to what they can practice and do.

Aura Reading – Understanding the basics and learning how to read and understand people's unique energy signature. *Such tools are good for beginners to learn and understand how to feel, operate, and strengths. (Auras are recognized by color variations that send out energy vibrations from what some call chakras. There are some individuals that have trained themselves to search out these auras and strong energies by reading auras. They call themselves psychic vampires and are known for feeding on the psychic energies of the individual. In this case this is like which many Sith try to master **"Force Drain."**

> **Blood Magicks** – A type of occult and sorcery practice which is used to either strengthen and enhance one's own energy and or to utilize one's own with another energy form, such as sigils and other workings.

Unlike the above-mentioned practices that allow you to feel energy, the force can best be reached through meditation. Once this universal spark is discovered it becomes easier to manipulate in time through yourself and even others. But one thing that must be noted is self-control and self-discipline no matter the route you take with learning to navigate these energies. Always remember that when working with energy or anything ritualistic there is a cost that must be answered to by the universe (You cannot get something for nothing.)

While the practices of the ISA Sith Empire do not always advocate some of the previously mentioned practices to summon or obtain energy, we nonetheless recognize that they are alternative methods to obtaining energy. And in respect of all of our readers I do not wish to go too far into that subject with this book at this time.

Unlike the above mentioned which are more veered towards pagan practices and sorcery using the force takes precedence on a different level. Though we both utilize energies, how we go about collecting and utilizing such is completely different. The force user will as the Sith Code dictates passion. The key to all is learning control and learning how to harness and feel the passion and the anger or any emotion inside of you. Any emotion anyone may feel at any given time leaves a trace signature behind. That is the very essence and energy of that emotion of how an action made you feel. Let us break down a scenario for learning purposes to better understand passion and the force and how to make it work for you.

SCENARIO ONE:

You have been married for a long while, several years in fact to the love of your life, everything you

ISA Eternal Brotherhood

feel like is perfect. Perfect life, Perfect house, dream car, dream spouse (be it handsome husband or a sexy wife) Everything is as it should be. You in fact just got back from a great vacation, nothing could be better. You go to work until you come back home, and you see a note.

Dear husband/ wife,

I left you for _____ that I met during our trip to Hawaii.

You go upstairs and all your spouses' belongings are gone including over half the savings in the safe. All this pain sends you into uproar, tears meet your face as anger spreads into your veins you let out a force scream. You feel venom coursing through your veins as you feel the sting of betrayal. **One foolish sith loses control feeling the venom (the heat) from the sting of betrayal.

SCENARIO TWO: In this scenario the same scene plays out perfect life, perfect spouse etc. The difference becomes is the control said Sith shows. Instead of losing immediate control he uses said passion and focuses on the emotion and energy he/she is feeling at the time and uses it. The venom that the Sith is feeling, that very burning feeling that fevers their very essence would be the energy we speak of. A Sith should use that and allow it to be stored inside of them to be used like a battery. That way the Sith can run off the charge when ever need be.

Any scenarios in life can be of consequence to a Sith, be it happy memories, sad, painful, fearful. It matters not. A true Sith knows the world is its oyster. Looking around at the world you know it is full of stories, emotions, and memories that people carry at any given time. It's not necessarily exploiting these to our advantage but knowing when to use such energy known to utilize the force.

MEDITATION

Many see meditation as something as a tool of the Jedi. This is not necessarily true as both the sides of the force see this as a focus tool. Meditation has a great multitude of benefits. How we manage to accomplish this is done differently for the two. Each of us has our own goals and desires we push towards. One of the first looks most look at for meditation regarding the Sith is Darth Vader and his meditation chamber.

Vader completed his meditation and opened his eyes. His pale, flame-savaged face stared back at him from out of the reflective black transparisteel of his pressurized meditation chamber. Without the neural connection to his armor, he was conscious of the stumps of his legs, the ruin of his arms, the perpetual pain in his flesh. He welcomed it. Pain fed his hate, and hate fed his strength. Once, as a Jedi, he had meditated to find peace. Now he meditated to sharpen the edges of his anger.

(Lords of the Sith – Chapter 1, Page 1)

ISA Eternal Brotherhood

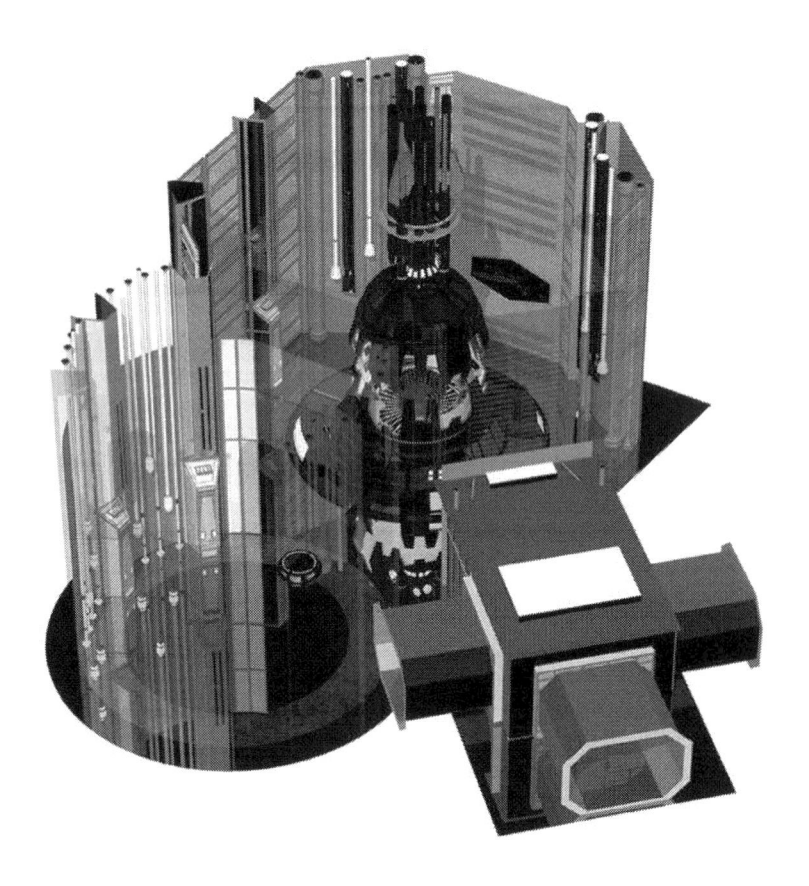

The Imperial Sithdom Alliances holds no copywrites to the above image.

One might wonder the sole purpose of meditation and what it can do for a Sith? The idea of meditation can be found throughout the history of mankind and many reasons for exploring this method of what many consider relaxation. But in honesty meditation can have multiple effects on how it can affect an individual, all depending on how one goes about achieving your goal.

What are the reasons and goals a Sith uses meditation?

Control
Drawing upon ones Emotions
Tapping into the Force

Control:
One of the most important lessons a Sith must learn. Because a Sith uses their emotions to draw upon their inner strength and those around them. It is key that a Sith must learn control. It is through self-control we can begin our training and mastering the environment around us. If we are to learn how to be masters of ourselves and our environment it must be said that we must learn to have control. The loss of control can cost a Sith much. Our energy and strength must be drawn from our

emotions, but without control we would allow our emotions to rule us instead of the other way, and the consequences could be detrimental.

Drawing upon one's own emotions:
If done correctly thru meditation one should be able to surface and draw their emotions on command. To do this one must focus on their day, think about their emotions and how certain events have influenced your mindset. Through quieting your mind and proper breathing techniques one should self-reflect on their personal decisions and events that have had any serious effects on them. By reflecting on these emotions, remember the feelings that you felt and allow the energy of those emotions to surface.

Tapping into the Force:
If all the steps are followed directly during meditation, and you can quiet your thoughts and properly store your emotions according for later use. If quieting one's thoughts to only reaches outward into the nothingness to where your thoughts and emotions roam if sensitive one should be able to hear or see things from another point of view. This can even act as a voice in telling you the best course

of action in future events or even dilemmas you have been facing.

MEDITATION 101

SUPPLIES?

Are supplies needed to help a Sith to meditate? Some would argue yes and the idea of music, an altar, or even candles may be brought up. But none of these things are necessary. The only true thing a Sith needs is themselves. Certainly, there are objects that may help calm one's mind, but they are not required. Even Lord Vader had a meditation chamber, but this served multiple purposes.

If you are new and candles or an altar help you focus, then you should do so. There is no shame in using such tools. There are many out there who have trouble focusing on such. Though if one does choose to use tools this does help to serve a purpose. Certain materials can be beneficial if you are new to the Sith or if it helps you focus or concentrate. Even an altar can be a useful tool, though not necessary. An Altar serves as a place of worship and a great way to direct energy if you are not yet used to doing so.

PURPOSE TO MEDITATION

Are supplies needed to help a Sith to meditate? Some would argue yes and the idea of music, an altar, or even candles may be brought up. But none of these things are necessary. The only true thing a Sith needs is themselves. Certainly, there are objects that may help calm one's mind, but they are not required. Even Lord Vader had a meditation chamber, but this served multiple purposes.

If you are new and candles or an altar help you focus then you should do so. There is no shame in using such tools. There are many out there who have trouble focusing on such.

HOW TO MEDITATE

Despite what some may say or think meditation is more than focusing on your darker emotions of anger and hate. As Sith we are actually encouraged to draw from all passions in life.

The idea to focus is to clear your mind and to focus gathering strength and the answers to your questions. Find a quiet location all to yourself, a place where you can calm the mind You can meditate in any fashion you desire whether kneeling or crisscross (cross legged) Either is okay as long as you are comfortable and can relax. Some may even repeat the code as a controlled method of focus and concentration. There is no shame in this.

If you are new to becoming a Sith it is suggested that you start with just five min learning to clear your mind and to focus. After you are comfortable with this then you should be able to extend your time to fifteen minutes morning and night. Morning, repeat the above and clear your mind and focus your energy your emotions. Use your ambitions for the upcoming day to guide you, your thoughts. Let your thoughts take hold of you and let your emotions come naturally. Now use your emotions to fuel your desires, let this act as a natural energy and focus on whatever is on your mind. Let your emotions and energy guide you through the meditation.

Evenings before bed, Same as above relax and clear your mind focus on your breathing. Let it remain steady, calm and relaxed. After you find your entrance point begin reflecting on your day. What had occurred. The feelings that arose within you throughout the day. Now use the emotions, the feelings that begin to surface and use such. Draw on these feelings and let them take on a life of their own. Use such emotions that you're feeling and let them surge with energy. Use this and reach out in your meditation. Let them guide you to whatever answers you may seek. You cannot just think on the day but allow your energy to take you to the moments that need reflecting on. Allow a natural state to flow through you.

Eventually you may advance and handle 30min each. Let the force show you the answers you seek.

END OF CHAPTER QUESTIONS

1.) What are the pillars which are described in the Sith code which can be gained?

2.) What do you hope to gain when finally taking an apprentice?

3.) Look at the Sith Code. What does it mean?

4.) Take time to reflect on a time in your life past or present and explore your passions. How did those passions affect your ability to handle the challenges that arose? What passions were the most helpful? Which were the least helpful?

CHAPTER 4:
SITH MARAUDERS COLLECTION

THE LIGHTSABER

"This weapon is your life."
~ *Obi-Wan Kabobi*

The lightsaber is a force wielders side arm. But as it is put into question rather constantly, "If one has the force why would there be need of a lightsaber?" In this section we will be reviewing the parts of a Saber, the psychological connection between a saber and its wielder, and why a saber is a useful tool even in our universe.

The lightsaber is said to be a Jedi's tool. But is it not the same for a Sith?

Indeed, it is. The only difference between a Jedi and a Sith with their saber is the way we deal with our confrontation. A Jedi's belief is that peace is always optimal and in reach and should always strive to be achieved whereas a Sith has a stronger grasp on reality and the knowledge that peace is a lie therefore some confrontations are not meant to be solved but ended. And sometimes confrontations can only be me through force.

A Sith understands and realizes a saber is a direct reflection of his or her own soul and for this reason is why we often choose the red blade. Not just because this is what is shown in the movies, but because it reflects who we are as a person, mirroring our inner conflict, pain, and anger that dwells deep within. And as a saber is also a reflection of ourselves it should also exist as an extension of our very beings. Once you own a saber and begin to train with it let it become a part of who you are, let your emotions flow into your practices and training sessions. Let who you are as an individual shine through your work and ability to wield a saber.

Though most everyone has seen the movies and seen how awesome a lightsaber looks, especially the sound and how the plasma blade ignites from the emitter and gains the power from the crystal chamber, but sadly in our universe that is not a thing. Our advances in technology and science are more limited than those of the films. So what good is a saber in this universe, it is not technically a real weapon, right? A reasonable argument that I have heard a thousand times, and this may be true on many points, that the lightsaber is not as deadly as a real bladed weapon. So let us go over the multiple reasons for owning a lightsaber in this universe.

1. The lightsaber is a reflection as well as an extension of the Sith who owns the hilt. And it should mirror the Sith and his or her personality.
2. The Saber can act as a practice tool for a real weapon.
3. It is a symbol of who we are and what we represent.
4. The saber is a sign of greatness and understanding in our ways.
5. The saber is often used to settle conflicts within the Sithist Community. Often when two Sith come to a disagreement that cannot be solved by words, they may choose to duel and let their strengths and knowledge be spoken by combat with a blade of a lightsaber.

6. A duel with a Saber may also dictate strength among Sith and their ranks and offer a demonstration of who is more powerful and fit to lead.

LIGHSABER MECHANICS

How does it work?
"On the same principle as my whip...
When you activate that stud on the hilt. It releases a beam of coherent which forms the sword blade."
~ *Den Siva & Lumiya*

A proper Sith should know as well as understand how to assemble a lightsaber and what this entails.

It should be the challenge of every apprentice to be able to properly design and create their ideal saber, this would speak to the individual Sith's desire and personality. "Remember the Saber is a direct reflection and extension of the Sith."

Let us now move into the construction and review the parts of a lightsaber, the side arm of a Sith.

The Exterior of the saber

The Blade Emitter

Star Wars Universe- The Blade Emitter was a lens at the end of the saber hilt which converted the energy of the crystal into a focusing point by use of heated plasma.

Our Universe- The Emitter is the focus point at which the LED is reflected into the blade by use of diffusion film. The Emitter is also known to some as a blade holder which is where one places the blade into the hilt and usually is tightened down with a retention screw.

The Pommel

Star Wars Universe- The rear or bottom end of a lightsaber which was made from a heavy metal which was used to hold in the guts or inner workings and circuits of the saber. In some cases, the pommel carried an extra power cell for the lightsaber. Also, for some Sith they would weaponize the pommel of the lightsaber with a claw or a sharp point that could be used in fights.

Our Universe- The pommel is used as a counterbalance point for the weapon and is where usually the speaker for sound effects are housed, in most cases the pommel can be removed on a saber so that an opening can be found to do work to the inner parts of the saber including the circuit board.

The Power Switch/ Activation Stud

Star Wars Universe- There are a multitude of ways a Power Switch was used and or was made into a lightsaber all which were used to activate the plasma energy blade from the hilt. The original switch was mounted along the hilt as a power button, lever, plate and other mechanisms. These worked as a simple on/ off activation for the wielder. Some of the other activations are as follows...

Trapped Grip activation was a modification added into the switch that only would recognize the wielder. If one who was not the wielder tried to activate the blade, they would become injured by an energy discharge that would be delivered through the hilt shocking the offender or doing far more damage than they expected.

Force Activation was a rarer way of activating a lightsaber, in this case there was no switch or any other activation key as the wielder only used the force to activate his or her side arm.

Locking Activator This was a useful mechanism that could be added into a power switch that allowed the wielder to lock in the blades energy from turning off even when the wielder was no longer holding the hilt. This activation stud was useful to the wielder in certain fighting situations if the owner of the lightsaber was to throw the blade in combat at his or her enemy.

Pressure Grip This activation was not a switch but placed into the grip of the saber along the hilt. The lightsaber would become activated as soon as it was picked up and would release its energy as soon as the saber was no longer being used.

ISA Eternal Brotherhood

IMAGES AND DIAGRAMS

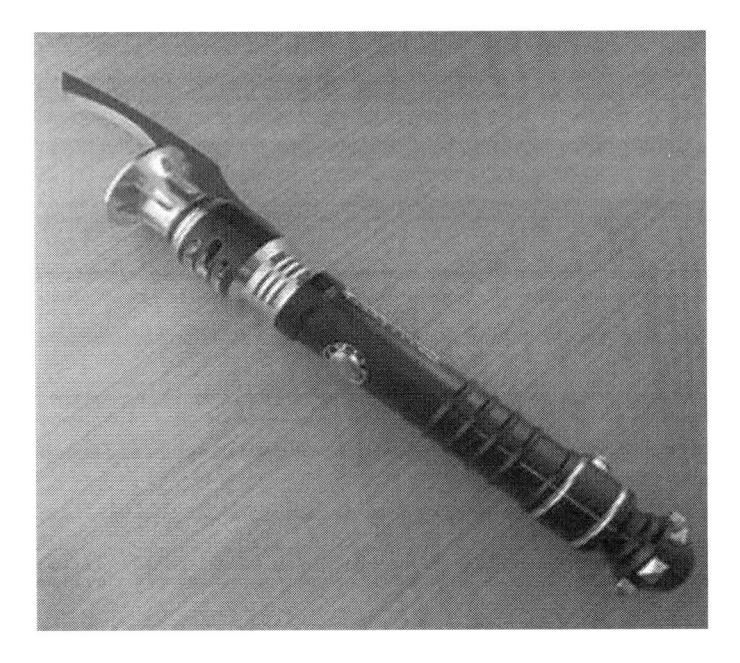

(Scorpion Lightsaber – Ultrasabers.com)

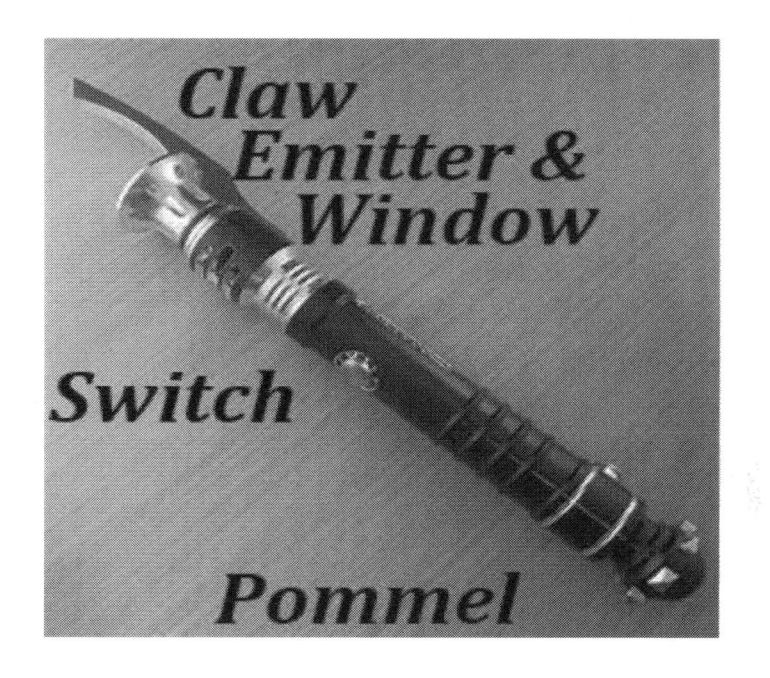

(Lightsabers hilt Labeled-Scorpion Ultrasabers.com)

ISA Eternal Brotherhood

INSIDE A LIGHTSABER

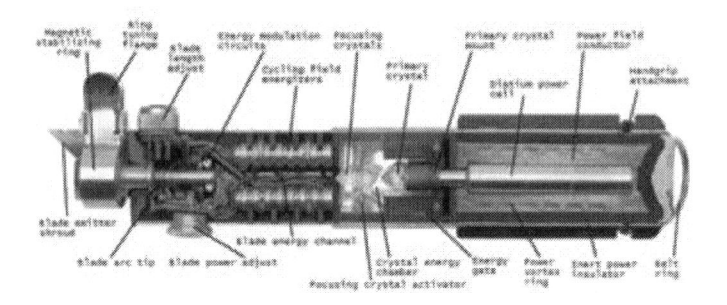

(Interior diagram of a Lightsaber per aminoapps.com and the Visual Dictionary of Star Wars)

ISA Eternal Brotherhood

LIGHSABER HILTS

Lightsaber hilts are known to have multiple facets and designs, such is often made to custom fit the desires of the wielder themselves. In many cases it is said to be a test and trial of a Sith apprentice to be able to forge and create their own lightsaber. What would your saber say about you?

Lightsabers have many kinds of styles that are used by their wielder such of those are
Standard, Double Bladed, Curved Hilt, Shoto, Light whip, Cross Saber, and the Dark Saber.

The Standard lightsaber hilt is the most common that you will see with a hilt that measures roughly 10-12inches long. With a blade that extends between 30in and 42inches. The length of the blade is best decided by how tall you are or the comfortability of a wielder.

The Double-Bladed Lightsaber is also known as a saber staff or a light staff. These double-bladed weapons have two blades that extend from either end of a hilt. Often these weapons can become two separate blades that attach and detach at a coupler to become two lightsabers. The blades are sometimes smaller on a double-bladed lightsaber for easier wielding.

The Curved hilt lightsabers are used by those that are more aggressive fighters that prefer a more offensive approach, using lunging and slashing techniques and those that like to feint against their opponents. Among the use of such Sith that have used a curved hilt is Darth Bane, Asajj Ventress, Dooku, and Darth Tyranus.

The Shoto lightsaber is miniscule in comparison to that of a standard, The length is nearly having the blade size and is made for younger sensitives or those that are comparative in size or smaller practitioners. Also, a shoto blade is a good choice for those who choose to wield twin blades. Such length makes the two blades easier to strike, often using one as an offensive and the other for defensive movements in a duel.

Light whip also known as a laser whip may sometimes be also referred to as an energy whip. This photon energy blade is much different than that of a straight blade used in the standard or other lightsabers. The distance that can be maintained by a light whip was traditionally longer than that of a straight which meant its control was harder to be mastered. This, weapon, was usually wielded by the Night sisters of Dathomir, a powerful group of witches/ sorceresses that could tap into the dark side of the force. This weapon took not only great control but finesse to wield and was a good way to cut, trap and entangle one's enemy. Among the Sith that wielded this weapon were Githany and Lumiya.

The Cross-guard lightsaber is a more ancient design of a lightsaber that was more commonly used, this design of lightsaber was created to ultimately protect the wielder from harm. The side vents known as quillons were used as vents to even out and the energy blade being emitted. This lightsaber was more commonly used by the Jedi and Makashi practitioners (second lightsaber form) As such there has only been one true notable Sith that used this weapon, Darth Atrius.

ISA Eternal Brotherhood

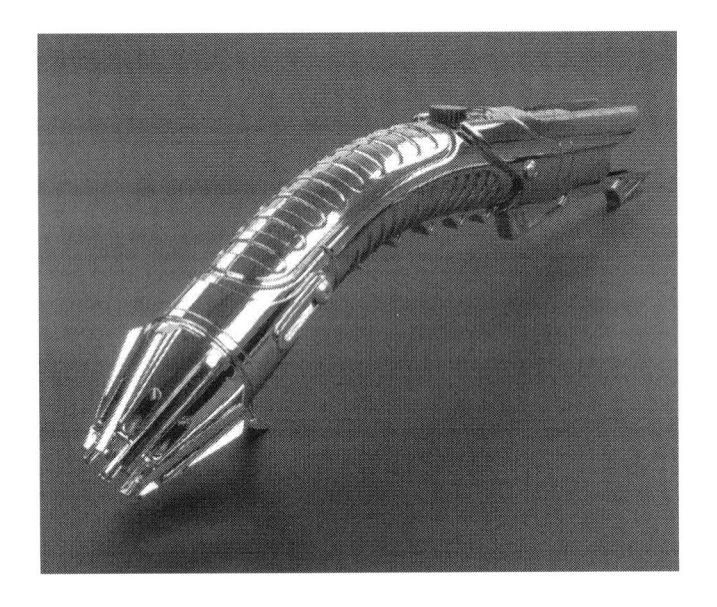

Imperial Sithdom Alliances holds no copywrites of the above image.
Curved Lightsaber hilt – product of SaberForge.

Imperial Sithdom Alliances holds no copywrites of the above image.
Crossguard lightsaber – product of Saberforge.

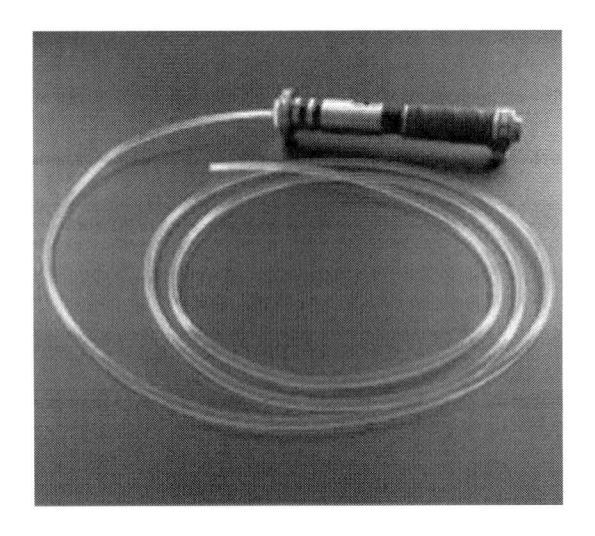

Imperial Sithdom Alliances holds no copywrites to the above image.
Lightwhip – Product of SaberForge.

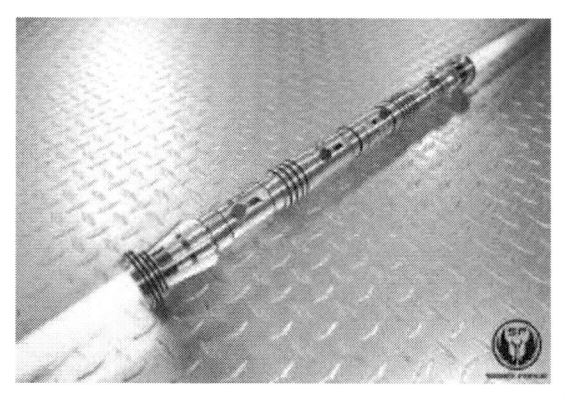

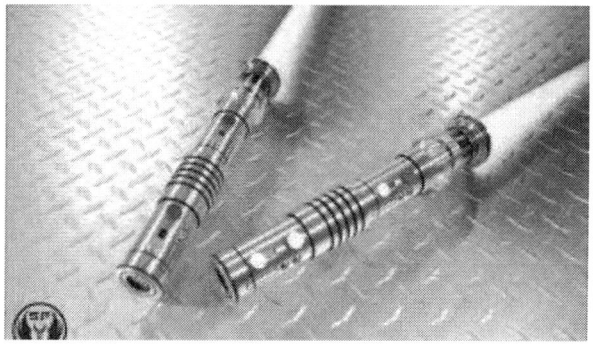

ISA Eternal Brotherhood

Imperial Sithdom Alliances holds no Copywrites.
Middle: Double Bladed Lightsaber
Bottom: Double Bladed Lightsaber dual bladed/ Product of Saberforge

ISA Eternal Brotherhood

Synth Vs Kyber crystals

There are a great many kinds of lightsabers that surround us. The lightsaber is the side arm of one who is trained in the force and is considered the primary weapon of a force trained being. Although many Sith chose to also carry other weapons they always keep a lightsaber at their side. Though the Sith and Jedi may both carry these elegant weapons there is a large difference, the crystal. Unlike Jedi light sabers that hold a natural kyber crystal a Sith's blade rejects them due to the nature of the dark side. A Sith would create and manufacture a unique synthetic crystal.

Kyber Crystals are known to have a natural origin resonating with the force and can be found throughout the galaxy though some areas were once more prominent such as the Crystal Caves on the planet llum. However, in 18 BBY the Galactic Empire destroyed the waterfall entrance to the cave barring others from entrance. Though over time much of the knowledge of the kyber Crytals have been lost, but one thing remains clear they are used in light sabers for their force properties to amplify and enhance the energy.

Synth Crystals are manufactured kyber crystals that are created by using a machine called a geological compressor. The geological compressor takes simple high carbon materials including the blood of a Sith and mimics the geological conditions from other planets on which force crystals are normally found and adapted to the proper settings. The blood of a Sith would be bled into the machine as it produced the crystal to give it the red hue and glow while the initiate or young Sith would wait for the process to complete they would meditate and focus their energies over it, embedding it with their ambitions and desires. It is for this reason that the synthetic crystal is known to be stronger.

ISA Eternal Brotherhood

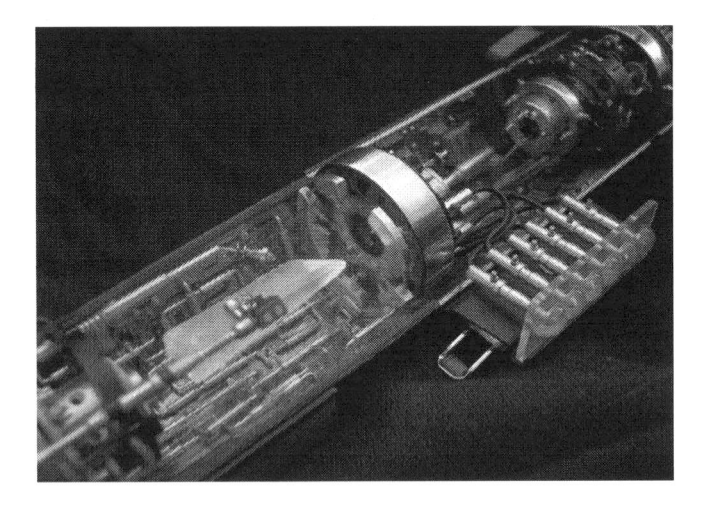

The Imperial Sithdom Alliances holds no copywrites to the above image.

LIGHTSABER FORMS

Form I
Shii-cho: The Way of the Sarlaac
Known as the Determination Form
Shii-Cho is used as the first form of seven and is taught to beginners.
Elementary in style and is used focusing on strike zones, parries, and blocks.

Form II
Makashi: The Way of the Ysalamiri
Known as the Contention Form
As your knowledge of lightsaber combat grows so do your forms.
Form two is a fundamental lightsaber form based on direct duels or lightsaber vs lightsaber combat.

Form III
Soresu: The Way of the Mynock
Known as the Resilience Form
A Contrast of the first two forms is made to create form three.
Soresu is based on defense for ranged or melee attacks.

Form IV
Ataru: The Way of the Hawk- Bat
Known as the Aggression Form
Ataru is designed to be a kinetically active form using one's entire body for high energy tactics.
This form relies on acrobatics and speed abilities.

Form V
Shien/ Djem So: The Way of the Krayt Dragon
Known as the Perseverance Form
Form Five is made up of two forms.
A combination of two forms
Shien and Djem So, form five was created to manipulate your opponent's attacks.
Shien: Redirects and counters an opponent's attack.
Djem So: focuses on saber dueling.

Form VI
Niman: The Way of the Rancor
Known as the Moderation and Diplomats Form
A conglomeration of all the proceeding forms one through five.
Niman is built on the mentality of the user instead of the weapon in his hand.
The user of this form should remain calm and collected.

Form VII
Juyo/ Vaapad: The Way of the Vornskr
Known as the Ferocity Form
Form seven rests its focus on attacks and zero defense. The form has its focus split into two separate forms
Juyo: Historically dates to the Jedi and Sith Civil War, the Jedi banned the teachings because its focuses purely on the attack and not on the defense. This form is a constant kinetic form relying on emotion to fuel it.
Vaapad: Youngest of the lightsaber forms and mastered by Mace Windu, Vaapad focuses on spin techniques and advancement strikes.

Enclosed, the ISA Eternal Brotherhood has enclosed their QR Code to offer easy access to their katas. It is our hope that this will allow for much easier access to practice at given time for whether yourself or perhaps your apprentice.

END OF CHAPTER QUESTIONS

1.) What is the psychological connection between a Sith and their lightsaber?
2.) Why makes the synthetic crystal stronger than that of a natural?
3.) Explain the process of a Sith using the geological compressor?
4.) Draw/ Work on and design your own skilled working lightsaber. Create one that has a significance to you and embodies who you are as a Sith.

HISTORY OF THE KATA

The idea for assigning a kata to each lightsaber form is similar to that of martial arts having a kata or a form for each of their belt levels. It is important to understand the principles and ideas are very old and date back to early China and is believed to have started during the Ming Dynasty.

Katas being rich in history are built with the idea to develop **MUSCLE MEMORY:** Repetitive movements for an improved efficiency and accuracy that is acquired through practice and repetition. Such katas were designed to develop techniques called **BUNKAI:** Analyzing or disassembling a kata for techniques and fighting movements. In doing so katas were designed to create more improved and focused methods of fighting skills through Bunkai to enhance methods such as strikes, blocks, parries, timing, etc.

Understanding and borrowing from a culture rich in understanding that started martial arts. The ISA Eternal Brotherhood looked for a way to help enrich and help young minds learn the forms associated with lightsabers. We want to thank

Chris McGill, a 3rd degree black belt for his help in developing such terrific katas, without his assistance none of this could have been possible.

CLOSING Sith QUOTE

"Being a Sith was not just about feeling hatred and anger; it was finding a way to focus those feelings toward the attainment of mastery."

~ Sean Willilams

~End Note~

In conclusion to the book, we do not desire to leave our Sith frustrated in disappointment, so we have decided to take imparting this knowledge in a different direction. While this book is all about divulging the information needed to assist in one's growth and development in the dark side as a Sith we recognize not all Sith pledge fully and only to the force and or to the darkness which resides in the force. Some practice another form, "Sorcery or the Occult" It is for this reason the ISA Eternal Empire will be releasing another book on such for those that desire to tread those more darkened waters.

Until then...
May the Darkness Guide you.